Original title:
Knobby Seams Over the Faerie Holl

Copyright © 2025 Swan Charm

Author: Johan Kirsipuu
ISBN HARDBACK: 978-1-80563-253-5
ISBN PAPERBACK: 978-1-80564-774-4

A Song of Earth and Ether

In the cradle of dawn's first light,
The whispers of earth take flight,
Beneath the soft embrace of trees,
Nature sings on the gentle breeze.

Colors dance in the morning dew,
A kaleidoscope of every hue,
Mountains rise with a stately grace,
Holding secrets in their embrace.

Rivers weave through valleys wide,
With stories of ages that they bide,
Each ripple carries a tale untold,
Chasing dreams both bright and bold.

Stars emerge as dusk descends,
A symphony that never ends,
With constellations that softly gleam,
Weaving magic in every dream.

As earth and ether intertwine,
Together they craft a world divine,
A tapestry of life we share,
Bound by wonder, love, and care.

Secrets of the Swaying Ferns

Beneath the shadows of an ancient grove,
Where whispered secrets dare to rove,
The ferns sway with a gentle grace,
Guarding tales of time and space.

Their emerald fronds, a soft embrace,
Hide the whispers of a hidden place,
Where spirits dance with fleeting light,
And dreams are spun into the night.

In every rustle, a memory stirs,
Of forgotten joys, of lost demurs,
The forest holds its breath and waits,
For all the stories time creates.

Mists weave through each time-weathered leaf,
Carrying with them a playful belief,
That magic blooms in the heart's refrain,
Helping to revive the lost and slain.

So heed the song of swaying ferns,
For in their dance, the world still yearns,
To unlock the mysteries they hold tight,
In the silence of the fading light.

Moonbeams on the Whimsical Trail

Under the canopy of a sparkling sky,
Moonbeams dance as the night drifts by,
On a trail where dreams take flight,
Laughter echoes in the silver light.

Whimsical shadows play upon the ground,
A symphony of night without a sound,
Each step unveils a magic unseen,
As stars twinkle in a cosmic sheen.

Through the trees, a lantern glows,
Guiding wanderers where the wild wind blows,
Nature's secrets beckon and call,
On this enchanted path, we rise and fall.

With every turn, there's a tale to share,
Of mythical creatures, beyond compare,
In the stillness, the heart awakens,
To the wonder that dreams have taken.

So follow the moonbeams, let them lead,
Down the whimsical trail where souls are freed,
In the soft hush of night's tender wail,
Let your heart roam on this wondrous trail.

Patches of Light in Dusk's Embrace

In twilight's soft and tender glow, Shadows stretch, the
night winds blow. A world transformed, as day takes
flight, Small wonders bloom in fading light.

Whispers dance in the evening air, Secrets hidden, a
gentle snare. Stars flicker, like dreams on a stream, Each
stitch of darkness weaves a gleam.

Among the trees, where silence sighs, Fireflies twinkle,
like borrowed skies. In the hush, all seems so right,
Nature cradles the heart of night.

A gentle breeze hums an old tune, While the moon sets
out to share its boon. Each moment lingers, a fleeting
spark, Guiding lost souls through the dark.

As night deepens, shadows blend, A tapestry woven,
without end. In dusk's embrace, the world will lead, To
places where the dreaming heed.

Echoing Footsteps in the Ferns

In dense green world, secrets unfold, Through whispers soft, ancient tales told. Each footfall echoes, a ghostly trace, In ferns that sway with gentle grace.

Sunlight dapples, a playful sprite, Guiding wanderers in flight. With every step, the past returns, In each heart, a wildness burns.

Beneath the leaves, a hush descends, Where time wanders and softly bends. Shadows weave where stories bloom, In the heart of the leafy room.

Nature's breath, a soft refrain, Calls the lost from joy and pain. In tangled paths, the spirit runs, Among the ferns and fading suns.

Every rustle, an invitation, To join the dance of creation. In the depths of the lush, we find, Echoing footsteps, ever entwined.

Murmurs of the Mysterious Glen

In the glen where shadows meet, Nature's pulse is strong
and sweet. Murmurs rise with the misty dawn,
Whispered tales of the night withdrawn.

Luminous glow of rising light, Dances lightly, takes to
flight. Over stones kissed by a stream, Breathing life into
every dream.

Ancient oaks guard the wayside, With gnarled roots and
hearts of pride. They murmur soft to those who dare,
Seekers lost, laid bare, laid bare.

Flora blooms with a vibrant voice, In every fragrance, the
heart will rejoice. Magic lingers in every sigh, As time
flows gently, like the sky.

In the glen, where wonders dwell, A tapestry too rich to
tell. Listen close, let your spirit blend, In the murmurs
that never end.

The Secret Life of Twisted Branches

Beneath the bows, where shadows lie, Twisted branches
touch the sky. They weave their stories, old and wise, In
knots that shelter whispered sighs.

Bark like skin tells of the years, Each wrinkle holds
forgotten tears. In their arms, the secrets stay, Of lovers
lost and dreams at play.

In gnarled hands, the winds will talk, With tales of paths
where no one walks. A symphony of rustling leaves,
Carries hopes that nature weaves.

In twilight's glow, the branches sway, Crafting magic that
will not fray. Ever watchful, they stand in prime,
Guardians of the forgotten rhyme.

A canopy rich with stories old, In twisted forms, the
dreams unfold. They shelter whispers of those who dance,
Amidst the branches, lost in chance.

Hidden Glades and Wandering Ways

Amidst the ferns, a secret lies,
Where ancient whispers touch the skies.
The sunlight spills like molten gold,
In hidden glades, where dreams unfold.

Through winding paths, the shadows dance,
A playful breeze, a fleeting chance.
With every step, the world anew,
The wandering ways invite the view.

A silver brook sings to the trees,
Its gentle laughter in the breeze.
Each footfall echoes, soft and light,
In hidden glades where hearts take flight.

The birds share tales of days gone past,
In melodies that ever last.
With every sigh, the forest breathes,
In wandering ways, it weaves and weaves.

So let your spirit roam and find,
The magic woven in the mind.
In hidden glades, let wonders play,
Upon the paths of wandering ways.

Fabric of Forgotten Lore

In twilight's grip, old stories dwell,
A tapestry spun with whispered spells.
Through pages worn and voices faint,
The fabric of lore, a mystic paint.

With shadows deep and candle's light,
The past comes alive in the still of night.
Each tale a thread, each legend bright,
Woven in dreams, lost from sight.

The creatures of old in whispers weave,
As memories spin, we learn to believe.
In folklore's arms, we find our way,
Through the fabric where shadows play.

Forgotten realms, where echoes call,
In the rooms of time, we rise, we fall.
Through ancient trees and broken stone,
The whispers of lore, forever known.

So linger here, dear friend of mine,
In the heart of tales, where stories shine.
For in each thread, a journey lies,
The fabric of lore beneath the skies.

The Silken Whisper Among the Leaves

In each soft rustle, secrets dwell,
A silken whisper, a magic spell.
Among the leaves, the stories flow,
Where gentle spirits come and go.

The emerald glade, a cloistered space,
Where light weaves tales with a tender grace.
A breeze carries laughter, light and free,
In the silken whispers of mystery.

The fluttering wings of stories untold,
Nestled in branches, gentle and bold.
The heartbeats echo, the leaves alive,
In the hush of twilight, where dreams thrive.

With every sigh, the woods awake,
In silken strands, the past we take.
A dance of shadows, a swirl of hue,
Among the leaves, the world feels new.

So pause and listen, let silence speak,
In the rustling tales, the answers seek.
For in the moment, the magic weaves,
A silken whisper among the leaves.

A Tapestry of Faery Light

In glimmering woods, where faeries flit,
A tapestry glows in the moonlight's wit.
Each twinkle a thread, each laugh a song,
In the dance of the night, where we belong.

With lanterns of glow, the stars play near,
A world of wonder, rich and clear.
The faery folk weave with nimble hand,
A tapestry bright, a dreamland grand.

Their laughter sprinkles like autumn rain,
In shimmering streams where calm remains.
Through petals soft and silken skies,
The faery light, a treasured prize.

In every corner, magic lies,
In twirling lights and whispered sighs.
A tapestry spun from love and grace,
In faery realms, we find our place.

So wander softly, let dreams alight,
In the arms of the night, where faeries invite.
For in this weave, enchantments play,
A tapestry of faery light, we sway.

Where Dreams and Nature Converge

In a realm where whispers blend,
The wildflowers sway, their colors send.
Beneath the boughs where shadows play,
Dreams take flight, then drift away.

Stars sprinkle secrets on night's dark veil,
Each twinkling gem, a story frail.
Rivers hum in gentle tunes,
As twilight dances with the moons.

Glimmers of hope in the morning light,
Awakening visions from the night.
Nature's heart, a pulse so true,
Where dreams and earth begin anew.

The Enigma in the Mossy Depths

Beneath the ferns, the shadows creep,
Whispers echo, secrets keep.
Mossy carpets, soft and deep,
Guard the tales that silence weeps.

Ancient roots in tangled embrace,
Hold the mysteries of this place.
With every step, a sigh unfurls,
Drawing forth forgotten worlds.

The lowly toadstools stand precise,
In the depths, where shadows entice.
Each glimmering dew, a knowing glance,
Invites the brave to take a chance.

Stitches of Magic through the Forest

In threads of gold, the sunbeams weave,
A tapestry where spirits cleave.
Through emerald leaves, the stories sing,
Of whispered spells and the joy they bring.

A flickering wisp, a glinting eye,
Guides the heart that dares to try.
With each rustle, the forest stirs,
In silent language, the magic purrs.

Stitches of wonder, sewn with care,
Binding the night with dreams laid bare.
As moonlight drapes its silver thread,
In the soft embrace, the world is led.

Veils of Mist in the Early Dawn

Veils of mist, so soft and light,
Kiss the earth at morning's sight.
In the hush, secrets blend,
As day and night begin to mend.

Crickets hush their evening song,
While echoes of night linger long.
The sun peeks shyly, a muted hue,
Greeting the world, fresh and new.

The dewdrops shimmer, like tiny stars,
Promising hope wherever you are.
In this moment, magic flows,
As the wind's gentle warmth bestows.

Reveries of the Twilit Meadow

In gentle hues, the twilight blends,
The lush green grass, where stillness bends.
Fireflies dance with flickering light,
Whispering secrets to the night.

A breeze carries stories long untold,
Of ancient dreams and hearts of gold.
Soft shadows play, a fleeting sigh,
As stars awaken in the sky.

The moonlight bathes the meadow fair,
A silver veil, soft and rare.
Here magic brews in every glance,
Each shadow a memory, lost in trance.

Echoes of laughter, sweet and low,
A place where time doth cease to flow.
With every whisper of the trees,
A gentle promise on the breeze.

So linger on this twilight dream,
Where all is more than what may seem.
In the twilit meadow, hearts can soar,
Beyond the boundaries of evermore.

Mysteries at the Giant's Foot

Beneath a hill, so grand and wide,
A giant's shadow, an ancient guide.
In silent watch, the earth does kneel,
Guarding secrets few can feel.

Whispers of giants, lost in lore,
Echo through time, forevermore.
Stones that rumbled with laughter bold,
In tales of yore, their stories told.

Amidst the grass, a glint does shine,
A fragment left, from hands divine.
Each footprint tells of journeys vast,
In quiet tones, linking the past.

The air is thick with dreams untamed,
Of battles fierce, none ever named.
What lies beneath this timeless dome?
A world of wonder, calling home.

At twilight's hour, the magic stirs,
As if the land itself prefers
To share its tales, both dark and bright,
Beneath the giant's watchful sight.

Fables of the Forgotten Dell

In a dell where shadows weave,
Lies a tale few dare believe.
Hidden from the sun's embrace,
Time stands still in this secret place.

Mossy rocks and willow's sigh,
Sing the songs of days gone by.
Every flower holds a thread,
Of fables whispered from the dead.

A winding path, with secrets laid,
Leads to a glen where fairies played.
With laughter ringing, lost in air,
Magic weaves through the stillness there.

Yet shadows linger, dark and deep,
Guarding promises they keep.
In the rustle of the leaves,
Lie the hopes of those who believe.

So venture forth, if heart be true,
For in the dell, awaits for you
A tangle of wonders and old regrets,
In the silence, the magic begets.

Songs of the Twilight Canopy

Beneath the trees, where twilight sings,
The canopy drapes with silvered wings.
Whispers emerge from cloistered heights,
Dancing softly in the fading lights.

Each leaf a note in nature's score,
Melodies echo forevermore.
In shadows cast by fading sun,
Dreams and wishes intertwine as one.

The branches sway, a gentle lull,
With every breeze, the heart does pull.
Crickets hum in rhythmic tune,
Serenading the rising moon.

Among the roots, the stories flow,
Of all who wandered, fast and slow.
In this twilight woven space,
Each heartbeat finds its resting place.

So linger here, let magic bloom,
In the twilight's gentle room.
For every song, though soft, sincere,
Echoes through the twilight clear.

The Forgotten Tapestry

In shadows deep, where dreams entwine,
The threads of old begin to shine.
Each tale stitched with care and grace,
A whisper lost in time and space.

Beneath the dust, the colors gleam,
A story wrapped in silent theme.
Faded hues that softly call,
Awaking secrets from the hall.

The hands that wove those ancient sights,
Still linger on, through days and nights.
A tapestry of hope and fear,
From long-lost hearts now drawing near.

With gentle touch, we grasp the truth,
Of love once held in timeless youth.
Forgotten threads of joy and woe,
In every fold, their shadows glow.

Together spun, they tell the tale,
Of distant shores where memories sail.
In woven dreams, forever stay,
The stories that may fade away.

Fluttering Between the Foliage

In whispered green where secrets lie,
The breezes dance, the leaves comply.
Little wings in sunlight beam,
Whirling through a vibrant dream.

The rustling sounds, a joyous tune,
As critters dart 'neath silver moon.
Delicate paths where shadows play,
Nature's breath in bright display.

A songbird's call, a fleeting glance,
In forest depths, we find our chance.
To wander lost, yet feel the grace,
Of fluttering hearts in this embrace.

Among the branches, whispers flow,
Of ancient tales the greenwoods know.
In every rustle, life awakes,
A symphony the silence makes.

So dance along, through leaves anew,
Embrace the magic found in view.
For in the subtle serenade,
Our spirits lift, our fears do fade.

Treading Softly on Faey Floors

When twilight falls, the faey play,
In hidden glades where shadows sway.
With cautious steps, we find our way,
On paths where dreams and wishes lay.

The moonlight peeks through leafy seams,
Awakening the night's soft dreams.
Elusive whispers, light as air,
Guide us gently, unaware.

On faey floors of mossy green,
A world awakes, unseen, serene.
With every soft and silent tread,
We step where wonder often led.

In glimmered light, the fairies twirl,
Around the bloom, their laughter whirl.
Each glance reveals a hidden spark,
That beckons from the shrouded dark.

So linger here, where magic dwells,
Among the trees, where silence swells.
Tread softly on this sacred ground,
For in their grace, enchantment's found.

The Dance of the Dews

At dawn's first light, the world awakes,
With tender drops that gently shake.
Each blade adorned in crystal sheen,
A morning dance, a sight serene.

They twirl and spin, like stars on grass,
As sunlight spills, their moments pass.
From leaf to leaf, their laughter rings,
A symphony that nature sings.

In whispered glades, the dews confer,
Their secrets shared in gentle stir.
Each pearl upon the petals bright,
An echo of the starry night.

Through tangled vines and fragrant bloom,
They weave their magic, dispel the gloom.
A fleeting kiss, a glowing sigh,
In every droplet, hopes comply.

So join the jest, let spirits soar,
Among the dews, forevermore.
In nature's dance, we find our way,
Through morning light, to greet the day.

Dreamweavers of the Dappled Glens

In glens where whispers softly tread,
Dreamweavers spin their silken thread.
With every stitch, a tale takes flight,
Painting shadows, dancing light.

Beneath the boughs, where secrets hide,
Magic swirls like a gentle tide.
Fairy laughter, a sweet refrain,
Echoes softly through the rain.

They craft the dreams from silver strands,
Threading wishes with tender hands.
Each heart that wishes finds their grace,
In the soft warmth of that place.

Amidst the ferns, the stories bloom,
Awakening joy, dispelling gloom.
Here in the glen, all fears set free,
In the embrace of harmony.

By moonlit streams, where willows weep,
The Dreamweavers guard the dreams we keep.
So close your eyes, let visions soar,
In dappled glens forevermore.

The Lure of Twisting Roots

Beneath the oak, deep shadows spin,
Twisting roots that draw you in.
A maze of whispers, secrets weave,
There lies a magic hard to believe.

Each gnarled bend, a story told,
Of ancient spirits, brave and bold.
They beckon softly, hearts in tune,
In the hush of twilight, under the moon.

With every step, the earth does sing,
Embracing all that they can bring.
A pull of fate, an urge to roam,
In the embrace of the forest's home.

Look closely now, see faces there,
In twisted roots, a crown of hair.
The laughter echoes, wild and free,
In this hidden grove, where dreams might be.

The lure of roots, deep and profound,
Calls to the soul, a magic found.
So heed the call, let wonder sway,
In the depths of night and the break of day.

Nightfall over the Enchanted Grove

As twilight drapes its velvet cloak,
Nightfall spreads a magic yoke.
Stars ignite in a shimmering sea,
Whispering secrets, wild and free.

The shadows dance on twilight's grace,
In the grove, find a sacred space.
A symphony of sighs and dreams,
Echoes of laughter spill like streams.

Mysterious lights, like fireflies,
Reveal hidden paths beneath dark skies.
The trees stand tall, guardians grey,
Holding wisdom in their sway.

In every rustle, a tale unfolds,
Of love and magic, adventures bold.
In the stillness, hearts intertwine,
Underneath the stars that shine.

Nightfall's kiss, a gentle balm,
Wraps the grove in soothing calm.
Where dreams take flight, spirits glide,
In the enchanted woods, we confide.

Glimmers in the Gloom

Through tangled branches, shadows creep,
In the gloom where fairies weep.
Yet glimmers spark in darkest night,
A flicker of hope, a glowing light.

The whispers call from depths below,
Stories long lost, fading slow.
In every corner, magic stirs,
Glimmers await where darkness blurs.

The moon's soft gaze, a gentle guide,
Illuminates paths where dreams abide.
Hidden treasures, waiting still,
To awaken hearts and bend their will.

As shadows dance and spirits sigh,
Glimmers twinkle in the sky.
So tread with care, and seek the spark,
In the silence of the dark.

For in the gloom, the light will bloom,
With every heartbeat, the magic looms.
A promise cast in shadows' roam,
In glimmers bright, we find our home.

Secrets Woven in Nature's Threads

In the heart of the forest deep,
Where the ancient whispers creep,
Lies a tale of the trees so grand,
Woven tight by nature's hand.

Moonlight dances on leaves so bright,
Casting shadows in the night,
Each flutter speaks a secret old,
In the language of green and gold.

Crickets chirp a gentle tune,
Beneath the gaze of the silver moon,
Nature's secrets breathe the air,
In every rustle, a silent prayer.

Beneath the moss and tangled vine,
Old memories twist and intertwine,
The stories held in roots that bind,
Are treasures for the curious mind.

So listen close to the forest song,
In its arms, you will belong,
For every whisper, every thread,
Holds the magic of what's unsaid.

Curiosities of the Murmuring Glade

In a glade where shadows play,
Curious creatures roam and sway,
Each step reveals a hidden sight,
In the dance of day and night.

Mossy stones and petals bright,
Bear witness to the soft twilight,
Where murmurs of the wind confide,
The secrets that the woods abide.

Bubbles rise in twilight streams,
Carrying the softest dreams,
Each ripple holds a story new,
Of wonder in a world so true.

Fireflies light the evening air,
With a glimmer of magic rare,
They weave patterns, spark and spin,
A tapestry where dreams begin.

So linger in this whispered space,
Find the joy in nature's grace,
For in each breath, you may uncover,
The wild heart of earth, your lover.

Magic of the Hidden Nook

In a corner where the wildflowers bloom,
Lies a nook that dispels all gloom,
Where time folds back, and hearts are free,
Whispering secrets to you and me.

Sunbeams filter through leafy crowns,
Painting shadows on ancient stones,
In this haven, the world feels kind,
With wonders waiting, intertwined.

The fragrance of earth after rain,
Calls to wanderers once again,
As soft as the sigh of a gentle breeze,
Inviting solitude among the trees.

Branches sway with a knowing grace,
Embracing all in their warm embrace,
Tales of courage from days of yore,
Echo softly from every floor.

Step lightly, breathe deep the air,
In this hidden nook, feel the care,
For magic whispers in every crook,
In the heart of nature, solace took.

Tides of the Ethereal Glade

In the glade where silence reigns,
And the moonlight dances on gentle lanes,
Tides of magic ebb and flow,
As if the glade itself does know.

Ripples form with a soft caress,
Carrying whispers of wilderness,
In every wave, a tender tale,
Of journeys taken, dreams that sail.

Stars twinkle through the leaves above,
Spilling secrets of moonlit love,
A symphony of nightingale's song,
Holds the dreams where we belong.

The world feels distant, time stands still,
As nature fills our hearts to thrill,
Each breath a potion, pure and sweet,
In the rhythm of nature's heartbeat.

So wander forth, let spirits guide,
Let wonderment be your joyful stride,
For in this ethereal glade so wide,
Magic lives in every tide.

Whispers of the Twisted Grove

In the grove where shadows linger,
Whispers dance with the breeze,
Ancient trees and secrets sing,
Their tales carried on the leaves.

Mossy paths entwined with wonder,
A shimmer glows in the dark,
Footsteps light, yet hearts grow fonder,
Guided by a hidden spark.

Twisted roots weave stories old,
Time stands still in this embrace,
Magic caught in hues of gold,
Lost souls find their rightful place.

Through the mist where fairies weave,
A tapestry of silent sighs,
Hope and dreams begin to cleave,
Beneath the vast and starlit skies.

In the stillness of the night,
Where whispered secrets intertwine,
The grove awakens, pure delight,
A sanctuary divine.

The Tapestry of Moonlit Paths

Upon the pathways draped in light,
The moon spills silver on the trees,
A tapestry of shadows bright,
Woven soft by every breeze.

Footsteps echo in the night,
As stars peek through the canopy,
Guiding dreams that take to flight,
On trails where hearts run wild and free.

Flora blooms with whispered grace,
Flickering glow of fireflies,
Magic thrums in every space,
Awakening the hidden sighs.

Each stone and root sings tales of yore,
Of adventures lost to time,
The moonlit paths forevermore,
Breathe the secrets in their rhymes.

In this realm where dreams collide,
The night reveals its tender glow,
Wanderers feel their spirits glide,
On paths where magic tends to flow.

Shadows Beneath the Woodland Canopy

In the woods where shadows play,
Canopy of emerald leaves,
The sunlight fades, but hearts will stay,
Amongst the tales the forest weaves.

Beneath the branches, whispers hum,
Stories linger, echoes past,
Softly strum the ancient drum,
In melodies that ever last.

Nature's pulse beats steady, strong,
Creatures dart with fleeting grace,
In this realm where souls belong,
They write their fables in this space.

Crickets serenade the night,
As starlit sparks ignite the air,
The world drips in pure delight,
Soft shadows weaving dreams to share.

In the heart of twilight's breath,
The woods enfold with gentle ease,
In loss, in love, in life, in death,
Nature's voice carries on the breeze.

Echoes of Enchanted Echoes

In twilight's grasp, the echoes gleam,
Through valleys deep and mountains tall,
Whispers weave a haunted dream,
Where every secret starts to call.

Moonbeams cast their silver net,
In corners where the shadows creep,
Memories lost, but not forget,
Awaken from their timeless sleep.

Listen close, the air holds fate,
Each rustle and each sigh replies,
A symphony of heart and weight,
Beneath the vast and starlit skies.

Through labyrinths of verdant past,
The echoes dance, they twist and twine,
A song of ages long amassed,
Breathes life into the shadowed vine.

In every whisper, tales arise,
Of magic spun and fables bold,
In enchanted echoes, secrets lie,
Woven deep in stories told.

Glistening Hues of Hidden Realms

In twilight's grasp, the shadows dance,
Where secrets bloom in whispered chance.
Emerald glades and sapphire streams,
Hold echoes of forgotten dreams.

Beneath the boughs where fairies play,
The moonlight weaves a silver way.
With every step on mossy ground,
A magic waits to be found.

In every rustle, soft and slight,
A tapestry of pure delight.
The air is thick with ancient lore,
And every nook holds tales galore.

Painted petals, vibrant bright,
Caress the heart with pure delight.
In hidden realms where wild things roam,
These sacred woods, we call our home.

So venture forth, let courage swell,
In glistening hues, let wonders dwell.
Behold the world beyond the veil,
Where every breath tells a tale.

Beneath the Glimmering Canopy

Under branches thick and wide,
New adventures wait to bide.
The whispers of the evening breeze,
Carry stories through the trees.

In dappled light, a creature peeks,
As playful shadows gently speak.
Beneath the stars' enchanting watch,
The night unfolds, a hidden notch.

With every bloom, a tale to tell,
In fragrant air, all is well.
A world where dreams and whispers meld,
Beneath this canopy upheld.

The nightingale sings her sweet song,
A serenade to all who long.
And fireflies dance like tiny stars,
Guiding hearts from near and far.

So linger here, let time erase,
The worries wrought on daylight's face.
In this enchanted, glimmering space,
A magic found, a sense of place.

A Tangle of Whispers and Dreams

In twilight's glow, the stories blend,
Where whispered wishes never end.
A tangle of dreams in starlit skies,
Awakens hope in sleepy eyes.

Through tangled vines and branches frail,
Adventures wait beyond the pale.
A flicker here, a sigh or cheer,
Each sound a heartbeat drawing near.

The twilight hums with secret grace,
In every nook, a painted space.
With every step, the shadows tease,
Of what could be with hearts at ease.

In moonlit paths, our wishes soar,
Beyond the realms we knew before.
For in the dark, a dazzling beam,
Awaits the brave to chase their dream.

So take my hand, let's break the seam,
And tumble through this tangled dream.
In whispers low, we shall believe,
That magic waits for those who weave.

The Lurking Beneath the Bark

In shadows deep where silence clings,
A world unfolds on secret wings.
Beneath the bark, life stirs and sways,
In hidden realms of misty haze.

The thrum of life is whispered low,
As ancient stories start to flow.
With every creak of timbered spine,
The forest speaks in voices fine.

With rustling leaves and murmurs bright,
A tapestry of dark and light.
What lurks beneath the earth's embrace?
A wonder found in every space.

The fairies flit, the shadows play,
Their laughter softens night from day.
The whispers call to those who dare,
To seek the magic woven there.

So heed the calls, the subtle spark,
And wander deep, beyond the park.
In mysteries that softly hark,
You'll find the truth within the dark.

Secrets Among the Vines

Beneath the weeping willow's sway,
The whispers of the leaves will play.
Hidden paths where shadows weave,
In ancient tales, we dare believe.

A tapestry of green untold,
With secrets wrapped in threads of gold.
Every twist and turn reveals,
The magic that the earth conceals.

In twilight's glow, the secrets bloom,
A dance of light dispels the gloom.
Among the vines where dreams entwine,
The heart finds peace, a sacred shrine.

Unraveling time through nature's grace,
In this enchanted, hidden place.
With wonder in each breath we take,
The world around begins to wake.

To follow whispers on the breeze,
And seek the heart of ancient trees.
Among the vines, we drift and roam,
In nature's arms, we find our home.

Shadows in the Glade

The moonlit glade, where shadows play,
Hides secrets both dark and gray.
Whispers from the midnight air,
Invite the dreamers, bold and rare.

Dancing lights that flicker bright,
Guide the lost through endless night.
In silence deep, the spirits hum,
A haunting song, both soft and numb.

Beneath the boughs where wishes hide,
The echoes of the night abide.
Each rustling leaf, a love declared,
In shadows gathering, souls laid bare.

Soft steps tread on fallen leaves,
Carrying hopes that never grieve.
In glimmering dusk, we find our way,
Through serpentine paths where nocturne sway.

The spirits dance, both wild and free,
In every whisper, a promise to be.
Within this glade, our hearts ignite,
Forever bound to the cloak of night.

Mystical Pathways of the Forest

Beneath the boughs of woven light,
The forest sings, a pure delight.
With every step on untamed ground,
A world of wonders can be found.

Twisting trails through emerald spires,
Where sunlight sparks and each heart fires.
Mystical pathways lead us home,
In the woods, we cease to roam.

The whispers call from deep within,
A dance of shadows, soft as skin.
With vivid dreams of realms unknown,
In nature's arms, we have grown.

Each turn reveals a tale anew,
Of ancient magic, wise and true.
Where spirits dwell, and wonders cling,
Among the trees, the heart takes wing.

In every breeze, the secrets blend,
The forest's heart our souls will mend.
In pathways carved by time's own hand,
We follow dreams across the land.

Echoes from the Hollowed Oak

Upon the hill, the old oak stands,
A keeper of the whispered strands.
In hollowed core, the echoes lie,
Of tales once shared beneath the sky.

Through twisted roots and ancient bark,
It holds the fire of every spark.
With every sigh, a story told,
Of love and loss, of young and old.

The flutter of wings, a gentle breeze,
Calls forth the past with tender ease.
Each rustling leaf a voice from days,
Where laughter mingles with the haze.

In moonlit nights, when shadows creep,
The oak stands guard, a vow to keep.
With every heartbeat near its base,
We find the magic in this place.

So lean into the hollow's breath,
And listen close to life and death.
For in this oak, the echoes flow,
A timeless dance we come to know.

Hidden Corners of a Magical Realm

In shadows deep, where whispers dwell,
A hidden place, where secrets swell.
Beyond the light, in twilight's grace,
Unseen wonders, we long to trace.

Among the trees, the moonlight weaves,
Crafting dreams through silken leaves.
A flicker here, a shimmer bright,
What magic stirs in the heart of night?

Through winding paths, where fairies flit,
And ancient stones in silence sit.
The stars above, a guiding scroll,
Their tales unfold, deepening the soul.

With every breath, the magic grows,
In hidden corners, where no one knows.
Each whisper calls, like a soft refrain,
Inviting hearts to dance in the rain.

So step inside, take a chance,
In this realm, let your spirit dance.
For in the shadows, light can gleam,
In the hidden corners, you will dream.

The Gossamer Bridge

A bridge of silk, spun fine as breath,
Suspended high, in dreams, not death.
With every step, the world expands,
As hope weaves tight, like gentle bands.

Through misty paths and starlit skies,
Where whispered wishes softly rise.
The gossamer flickers, a silvery thread,
Connecting hearts, where shadows tread.

Each footfall sings a haunting tune,
A melody caught by the curious moon.
As spirits dance, and shadows play,
On this fragile bridge, we find our way.

In twilight's clasp, enchantments soar,
As dreams take flight, forevermore.
Through glimmering night, we shall glide,
On the gossamer bridge, side by side.

So let us tread where the light shall blend,
Towards horizons where worries end.
For every step brings us anew,
Across this bridge, just me and you.

Echoing Lullabies of the Woodlands

In the hush of night, where shadows play,
The woodlands sing their lullaby sway.
With whispers soft, the leaves confide,
In cradles woven, where dreams reside.

The owls hoot low, a gentle chime,
Marking the passage of tranquil time.
Each rustle tells a tale of old,
Of secrets cherished, and truths retold.

Moonbeams dance on the silver streams,
Casting a glow on our sweetest dreams.
In every breath, the forest sighs,
Cradling hopes beneath starry skies.

As night unfolds its velvet cloak,
The echoes of laughter, softly spoke.
In this embrace, the world stands still,
While woodlands weave their magic thrill.

So close your eyes, let the night enfold,
In the echoing lullabies, tales unfold.
For in this realm, we are free to roam,
The woodlands gently guide us home.

Enigmatic Patterns of the Earth

In the earth's embrace, a quilt of lore,
Patterns unveil, secrets to explore.
From rippling waves to mountain peaks,
The echo of nature softly speaks.

A spiral shell, a petal's curl,
Whispers of magic in every swirl.
In silent dance, the petals unfold,
Tales of the ancients, waiting to be told.

Through tangled roots and wandering streams,
We unearth the fabric of our dreams.
The soil breathes life, both fierce and kind,
In patterns etched, our fate intertwined.

The dance of the stars, a cosmic rhyme,
Guides us through the corridors of time.
A tapestry woven, both bold and frail,
In enigmatic patterns, we shall prevail.

So walk with me through nature's grace,
Where every pattern finds its place.
For in the earth, our stories merge,
With enigmatic patterns, we all surge.

Legends in the Misty Depths

In shadows where the secrets lie,
Old tales whispered to the sigh.
Beneath the fog, the spirits creep,
Guardians of the dreams we keep.

A shimmering light breaks through the veil,
Guiding wanderers on a trail.
With echoes of a bygone age,
They turn the fables into sage.

The river sings a haunting song,
Where ancient hearts and hopes belong.
In every ripple, stories weave,
Of those who dared, who chose to believe.

Misty figures dance and play,
In a world that fades away.
With every step, the legends spark,
Illuminating the endless dark.

Where the Twilight Fables Slumber

Beneath the stars, where shadows rest,
Twilight whispers, a gentle jest.
In realms of dreams, the old tales bide,
Waiting for hearts to open wide.

Through glades adorned in silver hue,
Each fable spins in whispers true.
In slumber's grip, the stories stay,
Awaiting dawn to bring the day.

A nymph awakes with morning light,
To weave the fables into flight.
With every breath, the magic swirls,
In the world of dreams, the heart unfurls.

Where time is lost and hopes revive,
The tales of old come back alive.
In twilight's arms, they softly rest,
The slumbering whispers, tender best.

Visions from the Dappled Glades

In dappled light, the visions bloom,
Where nature dances, dispelling gloom.
Amid the trees, a story's spun,
In every leaf, a thread begun.

A tapestry of dreams displayed,
For dreamers lost, a secret glade.
Where sprites and shadows interlace,
And echoes linger, a warm embrace.

The gentle breeze, a soft refrain,
Entwines the heart with joy and pain.
In every sigh, a wish takes flight,
Guiding souls through day and night.

As twilight wraps the glades in gold,
The whispered visions bravely unfold.
From dappled paths, the stories gleam,
Where every heart can chase a dream.

Reflections in the Dreamweaver's Realm

In the realm where dreamers dwell,
Reflections weave their secret spell.
Mirrors glint with distant light,
Holding echoes of the night.

A tapestry of thought and time,
Where every shadow starts to rhyme.
Within the depths, the visions flow,
An artist's hand begins to show.

With whispers soft, the night unfolds,
A thousand stories yet untold.
The paths of fate, a winding stream,
Each twist and turn, a fleeting dream.

In the Dreamweaver's gentle hands,
The heart of magic softly stands.
Reflections dance, the truth reveals,
In every breath, the spirit feels.

The Life Beneath the Canopy

In shadows deep, where secrets keep,
The whispers dance, the branches sweep.
Creatures stir in emerald beds,
A chorus sings where sunlight spreads.

Beneath the leaves, the world awakes,
With tiny heartbeats, the forest quakes.
Mushrooms peek from the soil's embrace,
In every nook, a magic place.

The streams do twinkle, the flowers glow,
A tapestry rich, where wonders flow.
From tiny buds to towering trees,
Nature hums with gentle ease.

Each mossy stone, a story told,
Of hidden realms and treasures old.
The canopy holds the tales anew,
In the heart of green, where dreams come true.

So pause awhile, immerse your soul,
In life beneath, where we are whole.
For in the stillness, you may find,
The whispers of a world divine.

Unexpected Journeys among the Foliage

Through tangled paths, where shadows play,
A winding road leads us astray.
With each soft rustle, adventures call,
In depths of green, we heed the thrall.

A curious sprite, with laughter bright,
Guides us along in fading light.
With branches low and skies of gray,
We'll chase the dawn, come what may.

The leaves embrace our fleeting quest,
In whispered dreams, we find our rest.
Each turn reveals a hidden glade,
Where courage blooms, and fears do fade.

Beneath the bowers, a secret glows,
As fragrant petals dance like prose.
We leap through shadows, hearts in flight,
On unexpected journeys, pure delight.

With mirthful sighs and outstretched hands,
We weave our tale in twilight strands.
For every twist a chance to soar,
Among the foliage, forevermore.

Faery Footprints on the Wind

Soft echoes whisper in the breeze,
Of faery feet among the trees.
Tiny giggles, bright and clear,
A world of magic lingers near.

In twilight's glow, they flit and play,
Chasing shadows that dance away.
With shimmering wings, they trace the line,
Of dreams unfurled in starlit time.

Each footprint left on velvet air,
A promise made, a gentle care.
Through dewdrops glistening like pearls,
They weave their spell in silent swirls.

In moonlit glades, their laughter sparkles,
As night deepens, the heart's joyarkles.
With every breeze, a story spins,
Of faery footprints where magic begins.

So linger close, and keep your heart,
For faery whispers will not depart.
In dreams they come, on gentle wing,
Like softest tunes that night does sing.

Tales Woven in the Underbrush

In tangled threads of moss and vine,
The stories weave, both yours and mine.
From whispered leaves to rustling grass,
The past unfolds as moments pass.

An old oak stands, a wise old friend,
With branches strong, our dreams to tend.
It holds the echoes of laughter bright,
In the underbrush, a hidden light.

With every step, the tales reside,
In quiet corners where spirits glide.
A tapestry rich, with every hue,
From sun to rain, one thread shines through.

In secret nooks where shadows play,
The lore of life in green dismay.
Each story breathes through silence deep,
In underbrush, where wonders seep.

So let us wander, hand in hand,
Through meadows bright, a magic land.
For in these tales that softly thrush,
Our hearts are bound in underbrush.

A Dance Among the Ancient Roots

In shadows deep where secrets lie,
The ancient roots stretch down and sigh.
They twine and weave in silent grace,
A dance of time, a hidden trace.

The moonlight spills on forest floor,
With echoes of the days of yore.
Each step a story, soft and slow,
A whispering tide of long ago.

The leaves above sway high and free,
A rhythmic pulse, a lullaby.
Their voices blend, a symphony,
In harmony with earth and tree.

With every breath, the magic grows,
As starlight weaves through nature's throes.
A tapestry of life unfolds,
In vibrant hues, in shades of gold.

So heed the song of roots below,
Embrace the dance, let spirits flow.
In every step, in every glance,
The heart beats on, in ancient dance.

Beneath the Blooming Boughs

Beneath the boughs where blossoms play,
The world transforms, a bright ballet.
Petals drift like dreams in flight,
In whispers soft, they greet the night.

The fragrance wraps, a tender shroud,
Where laughter dances in the crowd.
Each rustling leaf tells tales retold,
Of summer's warmth, of days of gold.

A swing of joy on branches high,
Beneath the vast and watchful sky.
Children's laughter fills the air,
In blooming boughs, life blooms so rare.

With every glance, a story spins,
Of fleeting moments, of heart and sins.
The beauty found beneath the shade,
In every heart, a memory laid.

So linger here, let time be still,
Embrace the magic, feel the thrill.
Beneath the boughs, let spirits soar,
In blooming dreams forevermore.

Threads of Light in the Whispering Woods

In whispering woods, where secrets dwell,
Threads of light weave a charm and spell.
The sunbeams dance on emerald leaves,
Where nature sighs and softly breathes.

Each step reveals a hidden way,
Where shadows play and fairies sway.
The rustling grass, the croaking frogs,
Compose a hymn for wandering logs.

As twilight falls, the fireflies gleam,
In shimmering threads, they brightly beam.
A tapestry of night unfolds,
In shimmering whispers, stories told.

Beneath the boughs, the spirits gather,
In laughter shared, the night grows rather.
The moonlit glow, a guiding light,
In threads of silver, dark takes flight.

So roam these woods, let worries cease,
In threads of light, you'll find your peace.
Embrace the magic, feel the night,
In whispering woods, where all is right.

The Edge of Dreaming Ferns

At the edge where ferns begin to sway,
A bridge to dreams at end of day.
With soft green fronds that bow and bend,
A secret path, where dreams ascend.

The twilight whispers, calls you near,
With gentle sighs that soothe your fear.
Each curling leaf, a world unknown,
In ferny realms, the seeds are sown.

The air is thick with scents divine,
And in this realm, the stars align.
With every breath, the magic flows,
As starlit paths begin to pose.

In realms where wishes softly creep,
Beneath the ferns, the dreamers leap.
Embrace the night, let shadows twirl,
In dreaming ferns, let voices swirl.

So tread with care on gentle ground,
In whispered hopes, the dreams are found.
Let not the dawn break your delight,
At the edge of dreams, all feels right.

Harmonies of the Fae's Playground

In whispers soft, the fairies play,
Among the flowers, bright and gay.
They dance beneath the moonlit beams,
Awakening the night with dreams.

Each petal flutters, laughter swells,
In every shadow, magic dwells.
Their songs entwine with evening's sigh,
In twinkling light, the sparkles fly.

Around the brook, where secrets hide,
The fae with magic, side by side.
They weave the air with silver threads,
And cradle sleep on gentle beds.

A symphony of twinkling stars,
In glades aglow, and light from afar.
The night winds whisper, secrets shared,
In faerie realms, the world is spared.

With every note, the night enthralls,
In harmonies where silence falls.
Magic swirls, and dreams take flight,
In fae's embrace, all is right.

Unraveled Tales of the Green Thicket

In emerald depths, where stories breathe,
The trees conspire, the shadows weave.
Ancient whispers, lost in time,
Echoing softly, a silent chime.

The mossy stones hold secrets dear,
Of wanderers bold, and those who fear.
Beneath the boughs, the tales unfold,
Of courage, love, and treasures bold.

In thickets thick, where life abounds,
The heart of nature's pulse resounds.
A tapestry where legends blend,
And every leaf, a tale to send.

The winding paths, through sun and shade,
Invite the guests, both brave and fey.
Each footstep leads to realms anew,
In the green thicket, where dreams come true.

And as the sun dips low to sleep,
The stories wake, in whispers deep.
With every creature, every thread,
The thicket sings of souls long fled.

Shadows and Starlight in Serene Retreat

In tranquil woods, where shadows blend,
The starlight spills, a gentle friend.
It cloaks the earth in silver lace,
Enfolding all in soft embrace.

The owls call out, a haunting tune,
Under the watchful eye of moon.
Their wings brush past, like whispered sighs,
In silent dances, where magic lies.

Each step upon the forest floor,
Leads to a world, forevermore.
Where dreams take wing on twilight's breath,
And life unfolds in shades of depth.

The brook babbles tales of old,
Of secrets shared, of brave and bold.
In stillness found, the hearts unite,
In shadows cast, and starlit night.

Here time stands still, as souls entwine,
Beneath the sky, where worlds align.
In serene retreat, all worries cease,
In shadows and starlight, find your peace.

The Echoing Song of the Thickets

In thickets deep, where echoes roam,
A song arises, calling home.
With every note, the branches sway,
In harmony, they dance and play.

The rhythms pulse, like heartbeats near,
In ancient woods, both wild and clear.
Where nature holds her breath in thrall,
The song of life, it beckons all.

A symphony of whispering leaves,
In twilight's glow, the spirit weaves.
Each melody, a tale of yore,
Of magic held, and secrets' lore.

The creatures join, a chorus bright,
In twilight's hue, 'neath fading light.
The thickets sing, with vibrant glee,
An echoing song of wild decree.

And as dusk falls, the beauty grows,
In nature's arms, the magic flows.
A timeless bond, forever strong,
In every heart, the thickets' song.

Fables of the Hidden Vale

In the vale where shadows play,
Whispers dance the light away,
Ancient trees with secrets hold,
Tales of brave, of fears untold.

Moonlight weaves through branches tight,
Guiding lost souls in the night,
Each star a wish, a silent plea,
In this realm so wild and free.

Echoing laughter, a spirit's song,
Calls the wanderers, right or wrong,
Guardians of dreams in slumber's embrace,
Hidden joys in this timeless space.

Crisp leaves underfoot, a gentle sigh,
As faeries flit and softly fly,
Through glades adorned with morning dew,
Where fables find their life anew.

The sun will rise, and shadows bend,
Yet in this vale, the tales won't end,
With every dawn, a truth unveiled,
In the magic of the hidden vale.

Windswept Secrets of the Sylvan

In the forest, winds do roam,
Carrying scents of earth and foam,
Rustling leaves with a gentle roar,
Whispering secrets we can't ignore.

Branches sway in rhythmic dance,
Inviting wanderers to chance,
Aware of stories woven tight,
In the shadows that cradle night.

Mossy carpets beneath our feet,
Nature's chorus, soft and sweet,
Echoes linger, thoughts adore,
The hidden paths forevermore.

Moonlit nights, the stars align,
Glimmers of fate in each design,
Guiding souls through twilight's haze,
To find the magic in the maze.

When dawn arrives, the shadows flee,
Revealing nature's tapestry,
In windswept secrets of the sylvan,
Where dreams awaken, never givin'.

Echoes in the Emerald Shade

In the deep of forest green,
Lies a world unseen, serene,
Echoes flutter, soft and light,
Cradled deep in velvet night.

Glistening ponds reflect the sky,
As curious creatures flit and fly,
Moments stolen, shadows gleam,
In an endless woodland dream.

Gentle breezes tell their tales,
Carrying hope on wandering trails,
Where every footstep, every sigh,
Is a promise that won't say goodbye.

Cascading laughter, sweet and clear,
Lingers softly for all to hear,
In emerald shade, the heart takes flight,
Finding beauty in the night.

From every leaf, a story grows,
In whispers soft, the knowledge flows,
In echoes deep, let wisdom shine,
Through the emerald shade, divine.

Twilight's Veil of Mystique

As day gives way to evening's glow,
Secrets linger, soft and slow,
Twilight wraps the world in dreams,
Where nothing's ever as it seems.

Stars awaken in the vast expanse,
Inviting all to join the dance,
With shadows deepening their kiss,
A world ignited, a realm of bliss.

In the distance, an owl calls,
Echoing softly through woodland halls,
Guardians of the night take flight,
Bathed in the silver beams of light.

Alluring scents of pine and earth,
Whisper of magic, rebirth,
Each heartbeat sings of colors rare,
Under twilight's tender care.

Let us wander where the starlight veils,
Through the mist where wonder hails,
In twilight's grasp, the heart will see,
The mystique that sets the spirit free.

Mirth Among the Meandering Paths

In the woods where whispers play,
Laughter lingers, bright as day.
With every step, a secret found,
Joy blooms softly, all around.

The sunbeams dance on leaves of gold,
In stories rich and boldly told.
Bubbly streams in merry haste,
Invite us to their joyful feast.

Mirth wraps 'round like morning mist,
Each footfall bears a gentle twist.
Bright blooms giggle, sway, and twirl,
As nature's magic starts to unfurl.

Paths meander, twist and bend,
Mirth, a loyal, timeless friend.
With every turn, new glee is sown,
In this realm where love has grown.

Evening hush brings skies ablaze,
With memories of sunlit days.
In the heart where laughter dwells,
Mirth weaves its enchanting spells.

Vines that Speak to the Stars

In twilight's hush, a whisper flows,
From tangled vines where magic grows.
Each leaf a story, soft yet clear,
That speaks to stars we hold so dear.

They curl and weave, in cosmic dance,
Inviting dreams to take a chance.
With subtle grace, they touch the sky,
As if to ask the night to fly.

In moon's embrace, their shadows creep,
Where ancient secrets lie asleep.
They beckon softly to the night,
And bid the world to dream in light.

Through gnarled roots and twinkling eyes,
The whispers stretch, they rise and rise.
For in the stillness, hearts ensnared,
These vines of wonder have us bared.

Underneath their leafy shroud,
We find our dreams, both bold and loud.
In every twist, a path to fate,
Vines speak truths we'll celebrate.

Glowing Embers of the Twilight Glade

In twilight's embrace where shadows sigh,
Glowing embers dance 'neath evening sky.
With whispered warmth, they weave the night,
And cradle dreams in gentle light.

The glade hums soft with ancient lore,
While crickets sing and spirits soar.
Each flicker tells a tale untold,
Of mysteries wrapped in shades of gold.

Beneath the stars, a flickering glow,
Leads wandering hearts to secrets low.
With every spark, new hope ignites,
Transforming darkness into delights.

Embers twirl like fireflies near,
Igniting lives, dispelling fear.
The twilight glade, a sacred space,
Where freedom breathes and time we chase.

In this haven, all fears dissolve,
As glowing embers start to evolve.
With every heartbeat, magic, and grace,
The twilight glade finds its place.

An Intricate Lace of Nature

In nature's arms, a tapestry spun,
Threads of silver, under the sun.
Each blossom, a stitch, distinct and rare,
Woven in whispers, delicate care.

Branches intertwine, a graceful ballet,
While petals flutter, greeting the day.
In the stillness, each moment's embrace,
An intricate lace, a soft, warm trace.

Frosted whispers on morning's breath,
Nature's lace, a dance with death.
Yet through the chill, with warmth they blend,
A cycle of life, where beginnings mend.

The dew, a jewel on soft spun threads,
Holds secrets of slumber, where magic spreads.
In every leaf, a heart that beats,
Nature's lace, an enchantment repeats.

As twilight weaves its glowing hue,
Nature's lace whispers old and new.
In this woven world, we find our peace,
A timeless bond, where souls release.

Song of the Wandering Stream

Beneath the whispering trees, the stream flows,
Carrying secrets only the moon knows.
It dances over pebbles, sparkles bright,
A song of laughter in the silver light.

From banks adorned with willow's weep,
It sings of journeys, both wide and deep.
It weaves through brambles, wild and free,
A tale of wanderers, just like me.

In morning's mist, it softly glows,
In twilight's embrace, its melody grows.
The rippling waters, a gentle hymn,
A touch of magic where shadows swim.

Through fields of flowers and stones it sweeps,
In its gentle current, the heart leaps.
With every bend, a new story spun,
As it traces pathways kissed by the sun.

So hush now, listen to the stream's call,
For in its whispers, we are one and all.
It carries our dreams, our hopes, our schemes,
A lullaby woven from starlit dreams.

Spirits Among the Twisting Boughs

In the heart of the forest, shadows sweep,
Under boughs where the ancient spirits sleep.
Where the moonlight dances and whispers play,
Among the trees, lost tales drift away.

Gnarled branches cradle a flickering light,
The glow of the spirits ignites the night.
They weave through the leaves like a delicate thread,
Unraveling stories of those who have fled.

A chorus of whispers fills the cool air,
Echoing memories, both tender and rare.
In the stillness, life finds its voice,
Among twisting paths, we have a choice.

The roots of the past entwine with the new,
Where the spirits linger, their presence true.
In every rustle, in every sigh,
The heart of the forest will never die.

So wander softly, heed the call,
For within these woods, we rise and fall.
In shadows and moonbeams, find your place,
Among the spirits, you'll find your grace.

Luminescent Trails of the Night

Under the stars, the world is aglow,
A soft luminescence, a magical show.
As fireflies flicker, they weave through the air,
Painting the darkness with whispers of care.

Each step unveils a shimmering path,
Guided by starlight, in nature's bath.
The night unfurls mysteries, secrets unfound,
In the hushed embrace of the softly rounded.

With each twinkling dream, the heart ignites,
In the quietude dwells the world's delights.
Echoes of laughter, of love long past,
In luminescent trails, memories cast.

Through fields of shimmering silver and gold,
The stories of night are tenderly told.
The magic of twilight, a gentle embrace,
In the dreamscape of night, we find our place.

So wander the darkness, let shadows embrace,
In the luminescent night, discover your grace.
For in every twinkle, a promise shines bright,
A beacon of hope in the deep of the night.

Whimsy at the Water's Edge

By the edge of the water, where dreams take flight,
The world is aglow with spirals of light.
With laughter and echoes of whimsical cheer,
The ripples embrace the magic drawn near.

Tiny fairies dance on the surface so clear,
Sprinkling their stardust, creating good cheer.
Each pebble a canvas where stories unfold,
Of laughter and wishes and treasures untold.

In the soft morning sun, reflections abound,
Where playful secrets and joys can be found.
The whispers of nature, a soft lullaby,
Beneath the vast canvas of the endless sky.

As willows bend low, and the breezes play,
In the heart of the water, we drift and sway.
Each moment, a flutter, a pause, a delight,
In the whimsical dance of the bright morning light.

So gather your dreams where the water flows free,
For at the water's edge, there's magic to see.
In each vibrant ripple, a story is spun,
Of ports and of adventures, a life just begun.

Beneath the Mossy Canopy

In the forest deep where shadows play,
Whispers of secrets drift and sway.
Moss carpets dance on ancient trees,
Lulling the heart with a gentle breeze.

A brook murmurs tales of days gone by,
While silver stars twinkle in the sky.
Beneath the boughs where time stands still,
Dreams wander freely, as night winds will.

The moon casts a glow like a silken thread,
Waking the magic where once it fed.
A tapestry woven with moments rare,
Lies hidden beneath the soft, cool air.

Creatures emerge from their cozy nooks,
Guardians of legacies lost in books.
In their watchful eyes, a glimpse of lore,
A bond with the earth, forevermore.

So linger a while in nature's embrace,
Find solace and wonder in this sacred space.
For beneath the moss where all dreams belong,
Lies a world waiting, silent and strong.

Whispers of the Elderwood

In the quiet glade where old trees sigh,
Whispers linger like a soft lullaby.
Branches weave tales of the seasons past,
Echoes of magic, shadows cast.

The roots intertwine like stories untold,
Guarding the wisdom of ages old.
Beneath the canopy, secrets awake,
Each rustle and murmur, a path they make.

Moonlight filters through the leaves so fine,
Illuminating paths by design.
Here, time bends and dances in grace,
In the heart of the wood, find your place.

With every breath, the forest breathes back,
A rhythm, a pulse, a comforting track.
Listen closely; hear the trees speak,
In their deep voices, the answers you seek.

So wander these woods where enchantments lay,
Feel their embrace at the end of the day.
For in the elderwood, dreams come alive,
In every whisper, the wild will survive.

Enchanted Threads of Twilight

As twilight falls with a golden hue,
The world transforms, vibrant and new.
Stars peek first in the dusky light,
Each a promise of magic and flight.

Threads of shadow entwine the ground,
In hushed tones, the universe sounds.
The air buzzes low with stories of yore,
Waiting for hearts to open the door.

Glimmers of hope scattered like seeds,
In the cooling night where wonder leads.
Beware the spark of the twilight's kiss,
For it carries whispers of enchanted bliss.

A flickering lantern, a silky thread,
Guides you onward where brave souls tread.
In tangled paths, both wild and free,
Find the magic of who you can be.

So step into night with courage in hand,
Embrace the wonders of twilight's land.
For within each moment, a treasure glows,
In enchanted threads, adventure flows.

Tangles of Enchantment

In a thicket where wild roses bloom,
Magic dances in the sun's warm loom.
Vines twist gently, weaving a tale,
Of laughter and wonder beyond the pale.

Under the arch of the radiant sky,
Where dreams take flight, learn to fly.
Each petal a promise, each leaf a wish,
Whispers of fortune in nature's dish.

Starlit evenings glow with delight,
Painting the pathways where shadows might.
In spirals of ferns and secrets untold,
Tangles of enchantment in colors bold.

Listen to secrets the wind softly sends,
Stories of journeys that never end.
In echoes of laughter, find your place,
Tangled in magic, a warm embrace.

So wander these paths, let your heart roam,
In the tangles of enchantment, find your home.
For in every twist, a new story starts,
Weaving together the dance of our hearts.